Your Smile Makes Flowers Bloom

How the Core Competencies Can Help Children Thrive In Our World Today

JORDAN MAYER

WESTBOW
PRESS®
A DIVISION OF THOMAS NELSON
& ZONDERVAN

WestBow Press books may be ordered through booksellers or by contacting:

WestBow Press
A Division of Thomas Nelson & Zondervan
1663 Liberty Drive
Bloomington, IN 47403
www.westbowpress.com
1 (866) 928-1240

ISBN: 978-1-9736-8205-9 (sc)
ISBN: 978-1-9736-8204-2 (e)

Print information available on the last page.

WestBow Press rev. date: 01/15/2020

Dedication

For parents: You have the hardest job in the world. It takes a great deal of love and patience to raise a child. Often the things you do, big and small, go unnoticed. However, your words and actions are vital in helping your child thrive as an individual. Thank you for the time, patience, and energy you pour into your child!

For teachers: I believe you have the second hardest job in the world. You are required to engage a classroom full of children while dealing with countless distractions: fire drills, earthquake drills, spilled water bottles, spilled pencil cases, and phone calls just to name a few. You are doing an amazing job! Are you doing a perfect job? By no means! However, your work is valued and appreciated!

Contents

Prophets of a Future Not Our Own

It helps, now and then, to step back and take a long view.

The kingdom is not only beyond our efforts, it is even beyond our vision.

We accomplish in our lifetime, only a fraction of the magnificent enterprise that is God's work.

Nothing we do is complete, which is a way of saying that the kingdom always lies beyond us.

No statement says all that could be said.

No confession brings perfection.

No pastoral visit brings wholeness.

No program accomplishes the Church's mission.

No set of goals and objectives includes everything.

This is what we are about. We plant the seeds that one day will grow.

We water the seeds already planted, knowing that they hold future promise.

We lay foundations that will need further development.

We provide yeast that produces far beyond our capabilities.

We cannot do everything and there is a sense of liberation in realizing that.

This enables us to do something and to do it well.

It may be incomplete, but it is a beginning, a step along the way, an opportunity for the Lord's grace to enter and do the rest.

We may never see the end results, but that is the difference between the master builder and the worker.

We are workers, not master builders; ministers, not messiahs.

We are prophets of a future not our own.

Father Kenneth Edward Untener

Introduction

Children have a way of surprising us! They have the ability to make a statement so profound that it makes the hearer wonder how something so wise could come from someone so young. I had this experience while subbing at a small elementary school in my hometown. The classroom teacher had instructed in his lesson plan that students create a Mother's Day card. I introduced the lesson and handed out folded pieces of paper for students to work on. While making the cards, I helped students write familiar statements such as "I love you, Mom," or "Thank you for loving me." However, upon coming to a young boy's desk, I was taken aback. Written in small letters across the top of his card were the following words: "Dear Mom, your smile makes flowers bloom!"

What a beautiful statement! This child clearly felt free to express himself and play with language in a creative way. He didn't feel the need to write what was expected; instead, he took a risk and ended up creating the most profound Mother's Day card I have ever seen.

This is my hope for children living in our world today: that they would be equipped with the necessary tools to flourish in their homes, schools, and communities. Every child is unique and made for a purpose. As educators, we have the tremendous privilege of helping them discover their God-given talents and abilities.

The Core Competencies are carefully crafted tools that will help equip students with the skills, knowledge, and strategies they will need as they journey through life. I hope this book gives a glimpse of what the Core Competencies could look like through the eyes of a child.

I understand that this work in no way encompasses all that can be learned about this complex topic, however, I am committed to taking a small step to better understand the Core Competencies, discover how they can shape children, and learn how to help them thrive as individuals.

Core Competencies

What are Core Competencies? The Government of British Columbia defines them as "sets of intellectual, personal, and social and emotional proficiencies that all students need to develop in order to engage in deep learning and lifelong learning."[1]

To gain a better understanding of how the Core Competencies are organized, I would like to propose the following illustration. Imagine that there are three houses on a large piece of land: an orange house, a blue house, and a green house. Each house represents one of the three Core Competencies:

1. Communication
2. Thinking
3. Personal and Social

In the Communication house, there are two rooms, technically referred to as sub-competencies. The two sub-competencies are:

A. Communicating
B. Collaborating

The two sub-competencies for Thinking are:

A. Creative Thinking
B. Critical and Reflective Thinking

---

[1] Government of British Columbia, "Core Competencies," accessed June 27, 2019, https://curriculum.gov.bc.ca/competencies.

The three sub-competencies for Personal and Social are:

A. Personal Awareness and Responsibility
B. Positive Personal and Cultural Identity
C. Social Awareness and Responsibility

In each room, there are three or four bookshelves, technically referred to as facets.

The three facets of Communicating include:

1. Connecting and engaging with others
2. Focusing on intent and purpose
3. Acquiring and presenting information

From this point, I will go into greater detail within the facet of Communicating to demonstrate how the Core Competencies are further arranged; however the organization style pertains to all of the other facets as well.

Imagine that each bookshelf has six shelves, technically referred to as profiles. For Communicating, the six profiles are:

1. In a safe and supported environment, I respond meaningfully to communication from peers and adults.
2. In familiar settings, I communicate with peers and adults.
3. I communicate purposefully, using forms and strategies I have practiced.
4. I communicate clearly and purposefully, using a variety of forms appropriately.
5. I communicate confidently, using forms and strategies that show attention to my audience and purpose.
6. I communicate with intentional impact, in well-constructed forms that are effective in terms of my audience and in relation to my purpose.

On each shelf, there might be a single book or numerous books. The books on the top shelf contain elemental ideas, while the books on the bottom shelf are much more complex and advanced. This is to demonstrate how students begin with basic profiles and progress to more advanced skills through practice and purposeful reflection.

It is my hope that this illustration gives you a greater understanding of what the Core Competencies are and how they are organized. If you are having difficulty thinking of a way to introduce the Core Competencies to others, try the following activity:

Begin with a simple drawing of a person. Within the drawing, draw a heart to represent Personal and Social Competencies, a brain to represent Thinking Competencies, and a mouth and ears to represent Communication Competencies.[2]

Located at the beginning of most chapters in this book will be a Core Competency, and the chapter will explain how a child might encounter these competencies during a regular school day. For a complete list of the Core Competencies, see Appendix 1.

---

[2] Sandra Ball, "Self-Assessment of Core Competencies," *Starting With the Beginning*, December 7, 2017, https://startingwiththebeginning.wordpress.com/author/sandraball/.

1

A Bouquet of Flowers

Lucy woke up with a big smile on her face. Today was her mother's birthday! She jumped out of bed and ran downstairs to greet her mom and dad.

As Lucy dashed down the stairs, her gaze locked on a beautiful bouquet of flowers that sat on the kitchen table. The vibrant colours caught her attention, and she stopped for a moment to take in the beauty. Different shades of purple, pink, and yellow reminded Lucy of a sunset she had seen in Tofino the previous summer. Her mind flooded with warm memories, and she decided she would have to paint the bouquet on a canvas over the weekend.

"Happy birthday, Mom!" Lucy said, as she walked down the last few steps to the kitchen.

"Good morning, Lucy," Mom said. "Thank you for the beautiful flowers. They are stunning! I am especially excited to see the pink lilies open up later in the week."

"I'm excited, too!" Lucy said. "When Dad and I went to the flower shop, the florist said they should open in the next day or two."

For the rest of the morning, Lucy and her parents enjoyed a wonderful time together. They ate a delicious breakfast and talked about the crisp fall weather, the vibrant colour of the leaves outside, and the return of the salmon to local rivers. What an exciting time of year!

As soon as Lucy finished her breakfast, she cleared the dishes, placed her lunch kit into her backpack, brushed her teeth, and gave her dad a great big bear hug. "I love you, Dad!" Lucy whispered.

"I love you too, dear. Now, you better meet your mom in the car before you're late for school," Lucy's dad said.

"I know! See you tonight!"

2

Morning Check-In

Personal Awareness and Responsibility: I have some strategies that help me recognize and manage my feelings and emotions.

Emotional learning is not a quick or easy lesson. Many adults never master it. But practice makes better. The more practice young children get, the better they will be able to express their emotions and control their behaviour.
-Heather Shumaker

Lucy jumped into the backseat of her mom's car and buckled up. "I'm all set!"

"Let's roll!" Lucy's mom said, and they were off.

Lucy enjoyed morning car rides with her mom. Even though the ride to school was short, about ten minutes, Lucy relished the quiet time. Sometimes she would talk to her mom, but, more often, Lucy simply looked out the window. She enjoyed watching other people and looking out for animals. Lucy often saw a variety of birds, deer, and even the odd black bear!

As they approached the school, Lucy's mom asked, "What are you looking forward to today?"

Without hesitating, Lucy answered, "The joke of the day! Mr. Abiel always has a funny joke prepared for our class."

"That sounds like fun, sweetheart. Please tell me the joke when I pick you up later today!"

"I will!" Lucy said.

Upon arriving, Lucy said, "See you later!" to her mom, hopped out of the car, and walked through the front doors of Crystal Falls Elementary School. As soon as Lucy entered, she was hit with a wave of energy. Parents were busily talking to one another, students were eagerly waiting for the first bell to ring, and teachers were walking in a multitude of directions, completing last-minute preparations.

Although it was a busy place, Lucy took delight in the atmosphere. It made her feel like she was a part of something important, something bigger than her own little world.

At the sound of the bell, Lucy made her way up the green staircase to her second grade classroom at the top of the stairs. It was a treacherous journey, as students pushed and shoved to be the first ones in their own classrooms. However, after a few moments, things calmed down, and Lucy soon arrived at her destination.

Mr. Abiel was waiting just outside of the classroom door. He was a tall man wearing dark dress pants and a grey sweater. He had a bald head, big brown eyes, and a kind smile that warmed Lucy's heart. Upon seeing her, Mr. Abiel said, "Hi, Lucy! How are you this morning?"

Lucy answered, "I'm great! It's my mom's birthday today!"

"That's wonderful, Lucy!" Mr. Abiel said. "Please say happy birthday to your mom from me."

"I will!" Lucy replied, as they performed a secret handshake.

Secret Handshake Instructions

1. Shake hands and look the other person in the eye.[3]
2. Pound (Not too hard!)
3. Fishy (Pat the other person's forearm.)

---

[3] Kim Pallozzi, "I'm A Teacher And I Can See The Benefits Of Eye Contact In My Classroom," CBC, October 29, 2019, https://www.cbc.ca/parents/learning/view/im-a-teacher-i-see-first-hand-kids-arent-making-eye-contact-these-days.

Mr. Abiel did a handshake with the class every morning. Lucy didn't know why Mr. Abiel insisted on it, however, she was happy to participate. Lucy knew that Mr. Abiel noticed her, and without saying the words, he was able to communicate "I see you" in a powerful yet simple way.

After hanging up her coat and backpack, Lucy sat down at her desk to complete her morning work. She carefully took a blue one-inch binder from her desk and opened to a page titled "Morning Check-In."[4] Each morning, Lucy was to identify how she was feeling and explain why she felt that way. This morning, Lucy circled the happy face and wrote "I am happy because it is my mom's birthday!" Next, Lucy needed to pick a goal for the day. She decided to select "being a good friend," because she wanted to share the joy she was feeling with others.

Chapter Takeaway

Students need to have the opportunity to take responsibility for their physical and emotional well-being.

Core Competency Suggestion

Teach social and emotional skills to your students each day during a morning meeting or carpet time.

Thoughts for Educators

- Greet students at the door each morning, and perform a handshake with them. These handshakes can change each week or month.
- Students have physical and emotional needs that need to be met before authentic learning can happen.
- Keep a daily routine in the classroom. For example, during the morning meeting, begin by greeting one another, transition to a

---

[4] Lanesha Tabb, "Morning Work Binder for Empathy," accessed June 26, 2019, www.teacherspayteachers.com/Product/Morning-Work-Binder-for-Empathy-2495804.

song, and then end with the joke of the day. This routine builds safety in the classroom. Students understand what is expected of them, and can look forward to similar activities happening each day.

Thoughts for Parents

- Read stories with your child at home that touch on the topic of social and emotional learning. Brainstorm ideas for how your child can apply what he or she has learned in his or her own life.
- Keep a daily routine at home. This can create a calm atmosphere, encourage independence, and help your family bond.[5]

Suggested Reading Based on this Core Competency:

- *The Way I Feel* by Janan Cain

---

[5] Petit Journey, "10 Reasons A Daily Routine is Important for Your Child (and How to Set One)," Petit, January 10, 2017, www.petitjourney.com.au/10-reasons-a-daily-routine-is-important-for-your-child-and-how-to-set-one/.

3

Wooden Blocks

Creative Thinking: My play ideas are fun
for me and make me happy.

Play gives children a chance to practice what they are learning.
-Mr. Rogers

After completing the Morning Check-In, Lucy raised her hand to show Mr. Abiel her page. Mr. Abiel read it over, then told Lucy she could put her binder back into her desk.

Following this activity, Mr. Abiel typically allowed students to play at their desks. Lucy also enjoyed this time of the day, as it gave her imagination a chance to run wild. Toys such as wooden blocks, cooking sets, and Lego were stored in small plastic containers at the back of the classroom.

Lucy liked that these toys did not have to be used in a certain way. There was no right way to play with them; she could make up stories, pretend to be a chef, or create a skyscraper at her desk. It was quite a fun way to start the day!

As Lucy was walking over to the containers, another student named Violet appeared out of nowhere. She stepped right in front of Lucy and took the container that Lucy was hoping to take back to her desk. This frustrated Lucy; however, she was willing to let it go, at least for the morning.

Chapter Takeaway

Playing with toys that can only be used in one way decreases students' chances to think outside the box. Instead, toys such as balls, blocks, and dress-up clothes should be used to build a child's imagination.[6]

Core Competency Suggestion

Schedule time for students to play with carefully selected toys that will encourage creative and critical thinking. This could take place after morning work activities, during centers, or if students finish their work early.

Thoughts for Educators

- Rotate toys with your students. A small change can result in a lot of excitement!
- Sometimes, having too many options is not a good thing, so have just a few options for your students to select from.

Thoughts for Parents

- Try family play plans with your child during each season of the year.[7]
- Have a screen-free area in your home where children can play.[8]

Suggested Reading Based on this Core Competency

A Dark, Dark Cave by Eric Hoffman

---

[6] Teachers Resisting Unhealthy Children's Entertainment, *TRUCE Play and Toy Guide*, TRUCE, March 2017. www.truceteachers.org/uploads/1/5/5/7/15571834/ truce_play_and_toy_guide_2017_final_updated.pdf.

[7] Teachers Resisting Unhealthy Children's Entertainment, "Family Play Plans," accessed June 27, 2019. www.truceteachers.org/family-play-plans.html.

[8] Teachers Resisting Unhealthy Children's Entertainment, *TRUCE Play and Toy Guide*, TRUCE, March 2017. www.truceteachers.org/uploads/1/5/5/7/15571834/ truce_play_and_toy_guide_2017_final_updated.pdf.

4

You Know What Time It Is!

Creative Thinking: I can use my imagination to get new ideas of my own, or build on other's ideas, or combine other people's ideas in new ways.

When teachers use humor, students feel better about the content, the teacher, and even themselves.
-Robert J. Marzano

The class played with the toys for about twenty minutes before Mr. Abiel asked them to clean up. Once the toys were neatly away on the shelf, students were instructed to sit on the blue carpet for the joke of the day. Lucy sat next to her friend Ava. Ava was a quiet student who had short brown hair and large blue eyes. She wore red glasses, and had a way of making Lucy laugh like not too many other people could.

Sitting at Carpet Expectations

1. Sit criss-cross applesauce (sit with legs crossed)
2. Face forward
3. Raise your hand if you have a comment or question

"Okay, class," Mr. Abiel announced, "you know what time it is!"

"It's time for the joke of the day!" the students responded.

"My joke for you is the following," Mr. Abiel said. "What has four wheels and flies?"

Lucy's mind raced with possible answers. She thought maybe an airplane or a car with wings.

"A flying monster truck?" Tony asked.

"It's not a flying monster truck," Mr. Abiel said.

"What about the tooth fairy driving a convertible?" Linda suggested.

"Good try, Linda, but that's not the answer I'm looking for."

Six other students guessed before Mr. Abiel shared the answer. "Remember class, words sometimes have more than one meaning. These words are called homonyms. The key to answering today's joke was to think of an alternate meaning to the word fly. The answer to the joke is a garbage truck!"

"*Of course*!" thought Lucy. "*A garbage truck has four wheels and is often surrounded by flies because of all the garbage.*" She couldn't wait to stump her mom after school!

Chapter Takeaway

Kids love jokes, and teachers should too! Jokes help create a positive classroom environment, encourage students to think critically about words, and provide an opportunity to experiment with language.

Core Competency Suggestion

Have a joke of the day with your class, and encourage students to write their own jokes to share with you, their classmates, and parents.

Thoughts for Educators

- Humour is a wonderful way to keep your students engaged throughout the school day.
- Be careful when you use humour with your students: there is a time to be silly and there is a time to focus.

- Try creating a character who can show students unexpected behaviour (e.g. my character's name is Billy Bob Joe).
- Instead of telling your students, "You're wrong" when they give a confusing answer, ask "Why did you say that?" You may be surprised at the answer![9]

Thoughts for Parents

- Take time to listen to your child's jokes. They may be cheesy or not even make sense, however, your child will treasure the time you took to listen to them.
- Try creating your own character at home. For example, this character could be named "Messy McGee" and need help learning how to clean up. All of a sudden, cleaning just became a lot more fun!

Suggested Reading Based on this Core Competency:

Rosie Revere, Engineer by Andrea Beatty

---

[9] Danny Brassell, *Bringing Joy Back into the Classroom* (Huntington Beach: Shell Education, 2012), 16.

5

Lucy's Story

Communicating: I can communicate clearly about topics I know and understand well, using forms and strategies I have practiced.

"You can have brilliant ideas, but if you can't get them across, your ideas won't get you anywhere."
-Lee Iacocca

When the joke of the day was over, students were asked to do the following:

1. Find five other students
2. Shake hands
3. Look the other person in the eye
4. Say, "Good morning, (insert student's name),"
5. Go back to their desk for further instructions

Lucy started with Ava, then made her way around the classroom to greet four other students. This activity brought a smile to Lucy's face and she wondered, for a moment, why this might be. She remembered her mom talking about Love Languages[10] and how she had discovered

---

[10] Gary Chapman and Ross Campbell, *The Five Love Languages of Children* (Chicago: Northfield Publishing, 2005), 29-42.

Jordan Mayer

that physical touch was how she gave and received love best. A hand on the shoulder, hug, or handshake made Lucy feel warm and connected to the people in her life. Lucy also realized that looking at someone in the eye and hearing her name was a powerful exercise. Lucy didn't just feel noticed by her teacher; she also felt noticed by her classmates. Having other people acknowledge her helped Lucy feel comfortable and connected in her classroom.

After completing the activity, Lucy headed back to her desk and sat down.

Mr. Abiel said, "We are going to begin a writing activity. I would like to remind you that good writers present their information in a clear and understandable manner. When considering the 6+1 traits of writing,[11] this skill refers to *organization*. There are many ways to organize your writing: however, today we will focus on one skill. I would like you to have a clear beginning, middle, and ending to your story."

Lucy couldn't wait to get started! She wanted to write a story for her mom since it was her birthday. After sharpening her pencil, Lucy got to work.

Lucy's Story

One day, Mom woke up and decided to go on a bike ride. After pumping up the bicycle tires, she began her ride. However, Mom quickly realized that some of the flowers along the path had not yet bloomed.

She stopped and pondered out loud, "Why have only some of the flowers bloomed? It's the middle of summer and we have had plenty of rain and sunshine."

Much to her surprise, one of the flowers spoke: "Those flowers have not bloomed, my dear, because they need a different kind of light."

---

[11] A writing program that includes different traits that good writers use. See Ruth Cullham, *6 + 1 Traits of Writing: The Complete Guide for Primary Grades* (New York: Scholastic Teaching Resources, 2005), 100-133.

While my mom was thinking about the flower's statement, she noticed a small child playing with his dad at a nearby park. The dad was chasing his son through the park, and each time the child smiled, another flower opened up and displayed its beauty for all to see. As my mom rode home that day, she began to understand: the flowers didn't need more light from the sun; the flowers needed the light that shone through a person's smile.

Chapter Takeaway

Being able to communicate in a clear and understandable manner is a crucial skill for everyone to learn. It can be very frustrating to have an idea and not be able to explain it in a way that other people can understand. As educators, we must teach our students how to communicate effectively and provide several opportunities for them to fine-tune their skills.

Core Competency Challenge

Give students many opportunities to share their ideas with other people through writing assignments, science experiments, puppet shows, or Show and Share.

Thoughts for Educators

- We want students to take risks with their learning, e.g. teachers should not be spelling too many words for their students. When students take a risk with their spelling, praise their willingness to be brave.
- Everybody's best looks different, so try not to compare your students to one another.
- Try scheduling the subjects that require the most brain power in the morning, e.g. Math or English Language Arts.

Thoughts for Parents

- Work with your child to determine the best time of day for them to complete their homework. This will require some experimenting and a bit of patience.[12]
- Encourage your child to work on their communication skills at home. They could put on a magic show for the family or run a lemonade stand in the neighborhood.

Suggested Reading Based on this Core Competency

To Shy for Show and Tell by Beth Bracken

---

[12] Oxford Learning, "Day or Night: When Is the Best Time To Study?" Accessed November 18, 2019. https://www.oxfordlearning.com/best-time-day-to-study/.

6

Colour Tag

Critical and Reflective Thinking: I can assess my own efforts and experiences and identify new goals.

Without proper self-evaluation, failure is inevitable.
-John Wooden

Shortly after Lucy finished her story, Mr. Abiel announced, "We are going to get ready for gym class now. Please put on your gym shoes and line up at the door."

Lucy walked over to the coat rack, put on her neon runners, and lined up with her classmates. At the beginning of the year, Mr. Abiel had placed two lines on the floor: a blue line for the boys and a red line for the girls. If the girls were ready before the boys, they got to go first. However, if the boys were ready before the girls, they got to go first.

Line Up Expectations

1. Stand on the line
2. Face forward
3. Hands to yourself
4. No talking

Once the entire class had lined up, Mr. Abiel said, "The boys' line was ready to go first, so they will lead us to the gym. Remember when you get to the gym, you have two options; you can either jog around the basketball court or walk around the badminton court."

Mr. Abiel left the classroom and the boys followed close behind. As soon as Mr. Abiel was out of sight, Violet started talking to her friend Nicole. This frustrated Lucy, and she felt like she needed to say something.

"Violet," Lucy reprimanded, "This isn't the best time to be talking to Nicole."

"Mind your own business," Violet snapped, and without another word, she marched right past Lucy and down the stairs towards the gym.

Although Lucy didn't show it, she was quite frustrated and having a hard time keeping her composure.

"Don't worry about her," Ava said.

"Thanks," Lucy mumbled. However, that was easier said than done.

When Lucy got to the gym, she decided to walk slowly around the badminton court.

After a couple of minutes, Mr. Abiel blew his whistle twice and the class sat on a black line in the middle of the gym.

"Today, we are going to be playing a game called colour tag," Mr. Abiel said. "There will be four teams divided by colour: blue, yellow, red, and green. If I say that your team is it, your job will be to run around the gym, tagging your classmates. If you get tagged, you must freeze, and you can only rejoin the game if a student on your team gives you a high five. Before we begin the game, there are three things I will be looking for today: you are following the instructions, you are trying your best, and you are being kind to others."

Mr. Abiel handed out different coloured pinnies to the class. Lucy and Violet were both on the red team, while Ava was on the blue team. Once everyone had a pinnie, Mr. Abiel announced, "Green team, you are it!"

Immediately, everyone rose to their feet and started running wildly around the gym.

Out of the corner of her eye, Lucy realized that Violet had already been tagged. Instead of helping Violet, however, Lucy pretended she didn't notice and ran in the opposite direction. She felt bad, but reassured herself that someone else would help Violet.

When the game ended, Mr. Abiel asked the class to put their pinnies away and line up at the door. Before getting a drink of water and heading back to the classroom, Mr. Abiel asked each student to self-assess how they had done during the lesson.

Lucy remembered her goal from earlier in the morning: being a good friend. She knew that helping Violet was the right thing to do; however, she just hadn't wanted to do it. Lucy understood that she could not give herself a three, as she had not followed all three expectations outlined by Mr. Abiel, and was determined to be a better friend in the future.

"Lucy," Mr. Abiel asked, "what mark are you giving yourself today?"

"To be honest, Mr. Abiel, I think I deserve a two," Lucy said softly. "I followed the instructions and worked hard during the game, but I could have been a better teammate."

"Thank you for being honest," Mr. Abiel said. "I trust that next gym class you will be working on this."

Chapter Takeaway

Self-assessment is the linchpin of the Core Competencies. When our students learn how to use this tool properly, they will be able to take responsibility for their own learning and be able to effectively grow as individuals.

Core Competency Challenge

When completing self-assessments, students should always have an idea of what they can improve in the future.

Thoughts for Educators

- How long are your students sitting in the gym? They should be active for the majority of the lesson. Although this might seem obvious, try to be mindful of this the next time you are teaching a lesson in the gym.
- Challenge students with a next step when they complete a self-assessment activity, e.g. ask, "What can you do better in the future?" We all have ways in which we can improve and grow.
- As an educator, model self-assessment for your students, e.g. show your students notes that reflect on a lesson you taught. Show them what went well and discuss what you would change.

Thoughts for Parents

- As a family, get in the habit of reflecting at the end of each day. Ask, "What was the best part of your day? What was the worst part of your day?"[13]
- Encourage your child to keep a journal of their day. This could be done by drawing pictures or writing sentences.[14]

Suggested Reading Based on this Core Competency

Leonardo the Terrible Monster by Mo Willems

---

[13] The OT Toolbox, "Self-Reflection Activities for Kids," March 6, 2018, www.theottoolbox.com/self-reflection-activities-for-kids/.
[14] "Self-Reflection."

7

Buddy Bench

Social Awareness and Responsibility: I can tell when someone is sad or angry and try to make them feel better.

"Friendship is born at that moment when one person says to another, 'What! You too? I thought I was the only one.'"
-C.S. Lewis

When Lucy returned to the classroom, she changed back into her uniform shoes and sat down at her desk. Once everyone was seated, Mr. Abiel said, "Class, it is time to get ready for recess. I will see which group is ready first and dismiss those students to put on their coats and line up."

Sitting at Desk Expectations

1. Sit up
2. Hands folded
3. No talking

After dismissing each group, Mr. Abiel led the class outside to play in the designated area. Students ran in every direction. Some ran to a small playground and others played soccer.

However, Ava and Lucy had another idea. "Mr. Abiel?" they both said. "Will you chase us?"

Mr. Abiel chuckled, "Sure, I can chase you for a few minutes. You better start running or I'm going to catch you!"

Tag Rules

1. Mr. Abiel chases students who are playing
2. Once a student is tagged, all the students chase Mr. Abiel
3. The game continues until Mr. Abiel gets tired and needs a break!

Without another word, the girls took off. Ava ran towards the school, and Lucy headed towards a tall hedge on the opposite side of the parking lot. Mr. Abiel chose to chase after Lucy first. After a few moments, he had caught up with Lucy and gently tagged her on the back. Ava had noticed this, and soon both girls were chasing Mr. Abiel. In no time, they had caught Mr. Abiel, and he decided to try to catch Ava.

Finally Mr. Abiel said, "It's time for me to head inside. I hope you enjoy the rest of your time outside, girls!"

"Thank you, Mr. Abiel," the girls responded. "We will!"

Ava asked Lucy, "What should we do now?"

"I'm not sure," Lucy responded. "We could go play at the park. How does that sound?"

"Sounds like fun!" Ava said. "Let's go before the whistle blows and recess is over."

The girls started walking towards a small park located within the designated playing area, but they noticed a girl from kindergarten sitting on the buddy bench all by herself.[15] Without hesitating, both girls walked over.

Ava asked, "What's your name?"

---

[15] A buddy bench is a bench that students can sit on if they are feeling lonely. Other students can talk with this student or invite them to play a game. See Waynee Li, "Buddy Bench to Help Children Make Friends at North Vancouver

"I'm Clara," the student responded, without looking up.

"Are you okay?" Lucy said.

"I'm sad," Clara explained. "My best friend is at home today and I don't have anyone to play with."

"Oh," Ava said. "We were just on our way to the playground. Would you like to come with us?"

Clara nodded eagerly. "Yes, I would! Thank you."

Chapter Takeaway

A buddy bench is a win-win situation. It helps students who are feeling lonely find a friend and it teaches children how to show empathy towards others.

Core Competency Challenge

Role-play different scenarios with your students so they can learn how to recognize and include others who are feeling left out at school.

Thoughts for Educators

- Students are constantly saying "Watch me!" or "Chase me!" with and without words. Let's take time out of our busy days to notice children and play with them!
- Have students create a design for your school's buddy bench. They can paint the design onto the bench when they are done. (By the way, isn't children's art beautiful?)

Thoughts for Parents

- It is wonderful to have a best friend; however, students need to have the skills to interact with others when this person is not

---

School," CBC, March 30, 2016, www.cbc.ca/news/canada/british-columbia/buddy-bench-to-help-children-make-friends-at-north-vancouver-school-1.3512812.

Jordan Mayer

at school. Here are some suggestions for helping children make friends:

A. Introduce yourself, look the other person in the eyes, and smile.
B. Share interests and different things that you like and dislike.
C. Listen respectfully after asking the other person a question.[16]

- Encourage your child to notice others who are left out and lonely. Teach them how to show empathy and include others who may be feeling left out.

Suggested Readings Based on this Core Competency

- *Can I Play Too?* by Mo Willems
- *Have You Filled A Bucket Today?* by Carol McCloud
- *You Will Be My Friend* by Peter Brown

---

[16] Yanique Chambers, "Infographic: Teaching Children How to Make Friends," Kiddie Matters, accessed June 26, 2019, www.kiddiematters.com/ infographic-teaching-children-how-to-make-friends/.

Ribbon Rescue

Social Awareness and Responsibility: I can help and be kind.

Together we can change the world, just one
random act of kindness at a time.
-Ron Hall

As soon as the whistle blew, Lucy and Ava took Clara back to the front of the school to line up. They told Clara that she could play with them anytime and that they were looking forward to meeting her friend. After saying goodbye, the girls lined up with their class. Mr. Abiel led them back upstairs and instructed them to wash their hands, then eat their snack.

After washing her hands, Lucy walked back to the classroom. She sat down at her desk and pulled out a large banana from her lunch kit.

"Mr. Abiel," Lucy said. "Can you open my banana, please?"

"Yes, I can do that for you," Mr. Abiel said. "Which way would you like it opened today?"

Banana-Opening Options

1. Regular: Hold stem and peel the banana
2. Monkey: Peel the banana from the black tip towards the stem
3. Ninja: Hold the stem firmly and propel the banana downwards until it opens

"Can you open it like a ninja?" Lucy asked.

"No problem!" Mr. Abiel answered. With a quick flick of his wrist, Mr. Abiel snapped open the banana and handed it back to Lucy with a smile on his face.

After everyone was seated, Mr. Abiel announced, "Class, today I am going to be reading a story called *Ribbon Rescue*.[17] It is about a girl named Jillian who was given a dress with many ribbons. Throughout the story, she gives the ribbons away to help many different people. I don't want to tell you too much more. Let's start the story!"

From beginning to end, Lucy was enthralled with the book! She heard about Jillian giving away ribbons to help many people getting ready for a wedding: the groom, bride, best man, and even a family. However, after helping all of those people, Jillian was not allowed to attend the wedding because she had gotten her dress dirty. Instead, she was asked to sit on the steps of the church. While she was sitting on the steps, the bride and the groom found Jillian. They were so thankful for everything that Jillian had done that they made her the flower girl!

When Mr. Abiel finished, Lucy thought about the story for a few moments. It made her think of something that had happened a few weeks earlier at school.

The tape dispenser in the classroom was out of tape. Mr. Abiel was replacing the roll and asked the class if anyone wanted the white plastic roll for a craft. Many hands shot up, however, Mr. Abiel decided to give the roll to Lucy. At first, Lucy was thrilled! Her mind raced with many ideas of how she could use the roll to make a new creation. However,

---

[17] Robert Munsch, *Ribbon Rescue* (Toronto: Scholastic Canada, 1999).

after a few minutes, the excitement wore off and Lucy realized that she didn't really need the roll after all.

She remembered that Ava had also wanted to the roll and decided to give it to her instead. Ava was delighted that Lucy did such a kind thing and gave her friend a big hug. Lucy thought that for the rest of the day, Ava had been standing a little taller and smiling a little brighter.

Chapter Takeaway

Kids can change the world through small acts of kindness!

Core Competency Challenge

Challenge your students to find joy in giving things away, e.g. toys, items of clothing or money to a charity.

Thoughts for Educators

- Read to children as much as possible. At times, stories can be more entertaining than T.V. shows or games on tablets.
- Do not always explain the meaning of the story: let the power of story be enough.[18]
- Use silly voices when reading, e.g. a high-pitched voice for Piggy and a low, deep voice for Gerald the Elephant from the Elephant and Piggie series by Mo Willems.
- If you are not out of breath and sweating after reading a story, you might be doing something wrong!
- When reading to the class, give students an opportunity to be a part of the story; e.g. students can read the Duckling's lines while the teacher reads the Pigeon's lines from the Pigeon series by Mo Willems.

---

[18] Andrew Peterson, "He Gave Us Stories," Reformation Bible College, July 23, 2015, www.youtube.com/watch?v=mNC3UuDOCgs.

Thoughts for Parents

- Students do not always need to read books that challenge them or are above their reading abilities. Children need to fall in love with reading, and sometimes, that means reading books that may be below their reading level.
- Look at the statistics of the importance of home reading each day:
  A. Student A reads 20 minutes each day. This child will have read for 3600 minutes and been exposed to 1,800,000 words during the school year.
  B. Student B reads 5 minutes each day. This child will have read for 900 minutes and been exposed to 282,000 words during the school year.
  C. Student C reads 1 minute each day. This child will have read for 180 minutes and been exposed to 8,000 words during the school year.[19]

Suggested Readings Based on this Core Competency

The Smallest Girl in the Smallest Grade by Justin Roberts
Be Kind by Pat Zietlow Miller

---

[19] Kate Pereira, "Why Should My Child Read?" Motivating Minds, accessed June 27, 2019, https://mrspereirasclass.weebly.com/why-should-my-child-read.html.

9

Fun with Phonics

Positive Personal and Cultural Identity: I can describe and demonstrate pride in my positive qualities, characteristics, and/or skills.

Anything that is worth teaching can be presented in many different ways. These multiple ways can make use of our multiple intelligences.
-Howard Gardner

A few minutes after the story ended, Lucy and her classmates got ready for a phonics lesson.

"Today we will be learning about the sound 'sh' makes," Mr. Abiel said. "I want you to imagine that you are in the library and all of a sudden, someone comes in and starts singing very loudly. Can you visualize what you would do in that moment? If it was me, I would probably go 'shhhhh!'" Mr. Abiel scrunched his face and looked cross-eyed while making the sound.

The class laughed loudly.

"This is the sound that 'sh' makes in the English language. For example, 'sh' is used in the word shine, shore, and shiny. Can anyone else think of another example?"

"What about wish," Stanley suggested.

"Yes, that works!" Mr. Abiel said. "I like that you thought of an example where 'sh' is at the end of the word."

Six other students gave examples, then Mr. Abiel said, "Now that we have discussed the sound 'sh' makes, I want to give you an opportunity to show me what you have learned. You will have five options to choose from. With each option, you must think of words or items that contain the 'sh' sound."

Options:

1. Build it: Build a variety of items out of Play-Doh, Lego, or blocks
2. Write it: Write a short story
3. Sing it: Write a song and sing it for the class
4. Draw it: Draw a variety of items
5. Act it: Write a short script and perform a puppet play for the class

Lucy was very excited! She knew that she was too shy to sing or perform a puppet play, however, she felt comfortable drawing almost anything. She quickly got a blank piece of paper from the front of the classroom and began drawing a variety of things, including a ship, sheep, a shark, and a shell.

Before she knew it, Mr. Abiel was counting down to ask for the class's attention. "Three, two, one…hands on top," Mr. Abiel said.

"That means stop!" the class responded.

"Class," Mr. Abiel announced, "I want to give everyone a chance to share what they have been working on. Please clean up and we will get started."

Everyone tidied up, then Mr. Abiel asked, "Is there anyone who would like to share their work with the class first?"

"I can, Mr. Abiel," Ava answered.

"Great," Mr. Abiel said. "Please come to the front of the class and show us what you have done. Class, let's make sure we are showing whole body listening[20] while Ava is speaking."

Ava shared a short story with the class. It was about a shark who went shopping for shoes! It was quite funny and made Lucy giggle a number of times.

Next, Tony showed the class a shed that he had made out of wooden blocks. He was quite proud of his creation and excited to show everyone the floor plan that he had thought of complete with a kitchen, bedroom, and a fireplace!

After Tony, Nicole sang a short song in front of the class. Lucy was impressed! She didn't realize that Nicole could sing so well and planned to compliment her during lunch recess.

Several other students shared their creations with the class. Lucy smiled to herself as she thought about the lesson. It was neat to see her classmates present information in a way that made each person come alive.

Chapter Takeaway

Our students are gifted in many different ways. Let's give them many opportunities to show what they know in a way that makes sense to them.

Core Competency Challenge

Plan your lessons with multiple intelligences in mind.

---

[20] This concept refers to how we use different body parts when listening to others. See Elizabeth Sautter, "Taking a Deeper Look at Whole Body Listening: It's a Tool Not a Rule," Social Thinking, accessed June 27, 2019, www.socialthinking.com/ Articles?name=whole-body-listening-its-a-tool-not-a-rule.

Thoughts for Educators

- Challenge yourself to teach in a non-traditional way, e.g. teach a lesson outside or write a song for your students.
- Count down before you ask the class for their attention. This gives students time to stop what they are doing and prepare to give you their full attention.
- Students should be active when responding to attention-getters, e.g. saying a phrase, putting hands on their head, or clapping their hands. Here are a few examples for attention getters to use in the classroom:
  A. Teacher says, "Hands on top." Students reply, "That means stop!" and place their hands on their heads.
  B. Teacher says, "Sh, sh, sh." Students reply, "Sh, sh, sh."
  C. Teacher says, "Flat tire." Students reply by making the sound a flat tire makes.
  D. Teacher says, "If you can hear me, clap once." Students clap once. If needed, the teacher can then say, "If you can hear me, clap twice." Students clap twice.
  E. Teacher claps a rhythm. Students clap the same rhythm.

Thoughts for Parents

- Watch to see which intelligence(s) your child demonstrates. Encourage your child in this area throughout their life. Tell them that you believe in them and see this as a gift they can use to make the world a better place. The eight multiple intelligences are:
  1. Kinesthetic (body smart)
  2. Interpersonal (people smart)
  3. Linguistic (word smart)
  4. Mathematical (logic smart)
  5. Naturalistic (nature smart)
  6. Intrapersonal (self smart)

7. Visual (picture smart)
8. Musical (music smart) [21]

Suggested Reading Based on this Core Competency:

Randy Riley's Really Big Hit by Chris Van Dusen

---

[21] Tara Kunesh, "Multiple Intelligence Test for Children," LoveToKnow, accessed June 27, 2019, https://kids.lovetoknow.com/wiki/Multiple_Intelligence_Test_for_Children.

10

Building an Overpass

Collaborating: I work with others to achieve a common goal and can evaluate our group processes and results.

Alone we can do so little; together we can do so much.
-Helen Keller

Before math class began, Lucy and her classmates often participated in a GoNoodle activity.[22] In this particular video, an Olympic athlete would lead students through a warm-up and teach them how to compete in an event. Today, students would be learning about the 400 metre dash.

Lucy really enjoyed the videos as it gave her brain a short break before learning about a new concept.

Just before the video started, Mr. Abiel reminded the class, "Please use marshmallow feet when running in the classroom. We don't want to sound like a herd of elephants!"

When the video started, Lucy and the rest of the class completed a few stretching exercises, then they learned about a strategy for running the 400 metre dash. The Olympic athlete suggested running as fast as possible for the first 200 metres, maintaining a steady pace for the next

---

[22] GoNoodle is a website that contains a variety of fun videos that enable students to get up and move. See "GoNoodle," accessed June 27, 2019, www.gonoodle.com.

100 metres, and then going as fast as possible again before leaning over at the finish line.

When the video began, Lucy was ready! Along with her classmates, she ran as fast as possible. It was a ton of fun and, in the end, they were awarded with a bronze medal! When Lucy was asked to sit down for math class, she felt like she was ready to learn once again.

"That was a lot of fun!" Mr. Abiel said. "Thank you for running quietly during the video so other classes could continue to learn. We will now begin the math lesson. As you know, this month we have been learning about measurement. Today, I am going to be placing you in groups and asking you to build an overpass for a large vehicle. If you don't know what an overpass is, here are a few photos."

Mr. Abiel showed pictures on the screen, and Lucy remembered seeing an overpass last week when driving with her parents to Chilliwack on Highway 1.

"The large vehicle is twenty centimeters tall and ten centimetres wide. The overpass must be tall enough and wide enough for the vehicle to drive under. You will be permitted to build an overpass with cardboard, scissors, and tape, nothing else. Your group will receive a bonus point if the distance from the top of the vehicle to the bottom of the overpass is less than two centimetres. Before we begin the activity, I would also like to talk about being a good team member."

Mr. Abiel placed a poster under the document camera and began to explain what each letter of the word groups stood for.

G. Get along
R. Respect others
O. On task
U. Use quiet voices
P. Participate
S. Stay with your group[23]

---

[23] Nicholas Reitz, "GROUPS Poster," Teachers Pay Teachers, accessed June 27, 2019, www.teacherspayteachers.com/Product/GROUPS-Poster-1182282.

The explanation made sense to Lucy and she was determined to be a valuable team member during the activity.

"At the end of the project," Mr. Abiel continued, "you will be asked to assess yourself as a group member. Today, I really want you to focus on listening to other people and considering their ideas. You will give yourself a thumbs up, thumbs to the side, or thumbs down based on how well you are able to do this. I can take three questions before we begin and then I would like to get started."

Hands shot up all over the classroom.

"Go ahead, Sam," Mr. Abiel said.

"Can we use our scissors to cut the cardboard?" Sam asked.

"Yes, that is definitely okay," Mr. Abiel responded.

"Can we try the overpass after we build it?" Lisa said.

"That is the plan." Mr. Abiel answered. "We will bring the overpasses to the front of the classroom and test them out one by one. One last question."

"Can we take the overpass home?" Violet asked.

"Yes, however, you will need to decide with your group members who takes it home." Mr. Abiel said. "Okay, everyone, I will be placing you in groups of three. Once you have your group, you can get started."

When Mr. Abiel came to Lucy, he teamed her up with Nicole and Lisa. They got to work right away and constructed a well-built overpass together. A few times, Lucy needed to remind Nicole to stay with the group; however, for the most part they worked very well together.

At the end of the class, Mr. Abiel tested each overpass. Lucy and her group members were very pleased that their project was one of only two that received the bonus point. Before heading outside for lunch recess, Mr. Abiel asked each student to self-assess how well they had listened to one another. Lucy was satisfied with her efforts and decided to put her thumb up.

"Great work everyone!" Mr. Abiel said. "I saw some great teamwork today. Let's put on our coats and line up for recess!"

Chapter Takeaway

We need to teach children how to be a good group member. This is a difficult skill to master and takes a lot of time and a lot of practice.

Core Competency Challenge

Give students many opportunities to work with others and then have them self-assess their efforts after completing a project.

Thoughts for Educators

- Try to come up with expectations that students can envision, like "Can you imagine what it would sound like if you were walking or running with marshmallows on the bottom of your shoes?"
- When working on a skill, sometimes less is more, so instead of working on all of the skills at once, try focusing on one at a time.
- Brain breaks are essential in the classroom; they do not need to be long or fancy, e.g. touch each wall in the classroom, get up and give five people a high five, or transition to sitting at the classroom carpet.
- Try to be understanding and patient when students ask a question you have just answered. We all lose focus from time to time, don't we?
- You do not need to answer every question from every student before starting an activity. Students will most often figure things out on their own or they can clarify any confusion with their classmates. Try "I will take three questions and then we will get started."
- Have your students work with children they typically wouldn't choose to. This will help to build a positive classroom environment and give them an opportunity to make new friends.

- Try to keep numbers even between how many boys and girls you call on during classroom conversations.

Thoughts for Parents

- Encourage your child to be a team player and to look out for the interests of others.
- Incorporate brain breaks at home with your child, e.g. jumping jacks, running on the spot, or keeping a balloon in the air. Join your child in whatever activity they choose.[24]

Suggested Reading Based on this Core Competency

Franklin Plays the Game by Paulette Bourgeois

---

[24] Catherine Holecko, "Brain Break Ideas for Busy Kids," Verywell Family, accessed June 27, 2019, www.verywellfamily.com/brain-breaks-for-busy-kids-1257211.

11

A Tender Heart

Social Awareness and Responsibility: I can solve some problems myself and ask for help when I need it.

If we really want to love, we must learn how to forgive.
-Mother Teresa

When Lucy and her classmates got outside, they walked across the street to a nearby park, and Lucy thanked a parent volunteer who was working as a crossing guard.

The park contained a large playground, a soccer field, and various baseball diamonds. Earlier in the day, Lucy and Ava had decided they would like to play on the swing set during lunch recess.

"Race you there!" Lucy announced.

"You're on!" Ava said.

The two girls took off in high hopes of obtaining the only two swings; however, when they got to the swing set, Violet and Nicole were already using them.

"Hi, Violet and Nicole," Lucy said softly. "Just wondering how long you'll be using the swings?"

"Why do you care?" Violet snapped.

"We were hoping to use them today," Lucy said.

"Well, we're using them right now. You're going to need to find something else to do," Violet said.

"Okay, see you later then," Lucy replied. "Come on, Ava, let's go." The two girls slowly walked away.

"What's her problem?" Lucy asked. "She's been rude all day."

"Don't worry too much about it," Ava said. "Something might be going on that we don't know about."

"Maybe," Lucy said. "Come on, let's go play on the monkey bars."

After playing on the monkey bars for a few minutes, Lucy said to Ava, "Let's go see if the swings are free now."

The two girls walked over to the swings; however, Nicole and Violet were still using them. At this point, Lucy started to lose her cool.

"Violet," Lucy growled. "We've been patient and would like a turn now."

"No!" Violet said. "We got here first."

"Fine!" Lucy snapped, and began to walk away, but she quickly spun around and pushed Violet in the back. Violet fell hard onto the ground and began to cry.

In that instant, a giant rush of regret swept over Lucy and she bent down to see if Violet was hurt.

"I can't believe I did that, Violet. Are you okay?"

"Please just leave me alone," Violet begged.

"I can't do that," Lucy responded. "I did something wrong and want to make things right with you. I'm really sorry for pushing you, Violet. Can you forgive me?"

There was a long pause before Violet said, "Look, Lucy, I'm having a hard day. My dog, Pepper, is really sick and at the vet right now. Mom and Dad don't think she has much longer to live. I know I haven't been the easiest person to be around today, but I just wanted some alone time with Nicole. Yes, I do forgive you. Can you forgive me for being so rude to you today?"

"Of course I can," Lucy said. "I'm really sorry about Pepper. Can I give you a hug?"

"That would be nice," Violet said quietly. "Thank you, Lucy."

Chapter Takeaway

Conflict is a part of life and should not be avoided. Although it can be uncomfortable, conflict should be embraced and worked through. When this is done, it can lead to healthier relationships built on honesty and trust.

Core Competency Challenge

Teach your students how to apologize and forgive one another.

Thoughts for Educators

- Allow healthy conflict to exist in the classroom. Invite students to be honest with one another and have the opportunity to disagree with an idea or statement during a classroom discussion, which will lead to critical thinking and more creative ideas coming to the surface.
- Teach students how to solve problems on their own. Try the following ideas:
  A. Share and take turns, e.g. "Let's build a block tower together!"
  B. Tell them to stop, e.g. "I don't like how you are treating me. If you don't stop, I am going to talk to a teacher."
  C. Make a deal, e.g. "You can play for five minutes on the swing and then it will be my turn."[25]
- Take time to help students apologize and forgive one another. Try the following:
  A. Get down on your students' level, bending down or on one knee.
  B. Students should look one another in the eye.
  C. The student asking for forgiveness can say, "I'm sorry for…"

---

[25] "Kelso's Choice," Brownsburg Community School Corporation, accessed June 27, 2019, www.brownsburg.k12.in.us/Page/1287.

D. The student extending forgiveness can respond by saying, "I forgive you."

E. If the students are comfortable, encourage them to shake hands or hug.

Thoughts for Parents

- Instead of immediately solving a problem for your child, ask, "How can you solve this problem on your own?" Not every problem can be solved by a child; however, there are many things that children can accomplish on their own with a little perseverance.
- Teach your child the difference between tattling (a problem you could solve on your own) and telling (a problem that requires help from an adult).[26]

Suggested Reading Based on this Core Competency

Enemy Pie by Derek Munson

---

[26] matticeha1, "Tattling vs Telling Large," YouTube, February 25, 2012, www.youtube.com/watch?v=7H21_mkimkM.

12

Agendas

Communicating: I can understand and share basic information about topics that are important to me, and answer simple, direct questions about my activities and experiences.

I think the greatest challenge between child
and parent is communication.
-Sean Covey

For the rest of lunch recess, the four girls decided to play together. They pushed each other on the swings and tried to stump one another by telling as many jokes as they could remember.

"What kind of animal needs to wear a wig?" Ava asked.

"I don't know," Violet said. "What's the answer?"

"A bald eagle!"

"That's a good one," Lucy said. "What do you call a dog on the beach?"

"I know!" Nicole said. "A hot dog!"

The girls burst out laughing.

Suddenly, the whistle blew. Lunch recess was over and students were now expected to return to their classrooms to eat.

When the girls got inside, they washed their hands and started eating. Before leaving for his own meal, Mr. Abiel reviewed lunch expectations with the class.

Lunch Expectations

1. Remain seated
2. Use an inside voice
3. Put your lunch kit away when you are finished
4. Read or draw at your desk
5. One boy and one girl may use the bathroom at a time

During lunch, Lucy enjoyed talking with a girl named Brooklyn. They talked about math class and tried to guess what they would be doing for art.

"I think we'll be painting," Brooklyn suggested. "It's been a while since we've used our paint sets."

"That's true," Lucy said. "But I think we'll be drawing."

Soon the bell rang and Mr. Abiel returned to the classroom. He announced, "Please put your lunch kits away and take out a sharp pencil. We are going to be writing in our agendas. I kindly ask Tony, Bob, Lisa, and Brooklyn to help me distribute the agendas to the class."

When Lucy received her agenda, she opened it up and got ready to write a message.

"Can anyone tell me what we did for math class today?" Mr. Abiel asked. A few hands shot up in the air. "Go ahead, Sam."

"Well, we made an overpass." Sam said. "It needed to be tall and large enough so a truck could fit under it."

"That's right!" Mr. Abiel replied. "In your agenda, I would like you to write the following: 'Ask me about math class.' When you get home tonight, remember to tell your parents about your project."

Lucy quickly wrote the message into her agenda and then raised her hand. Mr. Abiel made his way over to Lucy's desk and checked the message.

"This looks good, Lucy!" Mr. Abiel said. "Just one thing; don't forget to put a period at the end of your sentence."

"Oops!" Lucy said, quickly placing a period at the end of the message. "I had forgotten about that!"

Before moving to the next student, Mr. Abiel drew a smiley face using check marks as the eyes. This indicated that everything was correct and Lucy could put her agenda into her backpack and get ready for art class.

Chapter Takeaway

As educators, we want to encourage our students to share as much of their educational experiences with their parents as possible.

Core Competency Challenge

Try to think of creative agenda messages that result in fruitful conversation at home. "Ask me about _____" is a good place to start!

Thoughts for Educators

- Give your students jobs in the classroom. You might be surprised how eager they are to help and how trustworthy they can be when given responsibility.
- Use a variety of means to share your students' learning with their parents/guardians. There are several websites and apps that enable educators to take pictures or videos to document learning and educational experiences, e.g. Seesaw and FreshGrade.

Thoughts for parents:

- Instead of asking your child, "How was your day?" try asking: "Who made you smile today?"
"Did you say thank you to anyone today?"
"What is something that challenged you today?"

"How were you brave today?"

"Did you learn any new words today?"[27]

Suggested Reading Based on this Core Competency

Franklin Goes to School by Paulette Bourgeois

---

[27] Leslie Means, "50 Questions To Ask Your Kids Instead Of Asking How Was Your Day," Her View from Home, accessed June 27, 2019, https://herviewfromhome. com/50-questions-to-ask-your-kids-instead-of-asking-how-was-your-day/.

13

Art is Messy

Creative Thinking: My creative ideas are
often a form of self-expression for me.

My sense is that conveying to a child a sense of
autonomy, and a feeling that what they were doing was
something they chose and they wanted to pursue, does
correlate with happy productivity and exploration
-Ann Hulbert

Once everyone had put their agendas away, Mr. Abiel announced,
"We are going to begin art class now. For today's lesson, we will be
completing a fish painting!"

Lucy and Brooklyn locked eyes and grinned. "You were right!" Lucy
whispered.

"Before we begin the lesson, I would like to introduce you to a very
special guest," Mr. Abiel said.

An older gentleman walked through the door and waved at the
students. He had wavy white hair and wore a plaid shirt with denim
overalls.

"Class, this is Mr. Cooper. He is a dear friend of mine and a very
talented artist. He has agreed to come into our school and lead you

through a project that you can take home later this week. Let's give Mr. Cooper a round of applause to welcome him to our classroom!"

The class clapped loudly.

"Thank you!" Mr. Cooper said. "It is a privilege to be here and I'm looking forward to a fun afternoon with you!"

"At this time," Mr. Cooper continued, "I would like you to take everything off of your desk. Your water bottles can also go on the floor, so they do not accidentally spill on your painting."

"For our painting today, we will be using stamps. Mr. Abiel and I have made Styrofoam cutouts of different species of fish. These Styrofoam stamps have wooden handles on the back of them, which you will need to hold while painting and placing the stamps on your acrylic paper. Each one of you will have an opportunity to paint on two or three of them. When you are finished with the stamps, you can add a variety of details to your painting. For example, you could add seaweed, bubbles, or even pebbles. You will have a lot of freedom with this project today. Try to be as creative as possible!"

Mr. Cooper and Mr. Abiel started handing out large pieces of acrylic paper. Lucy immediately wrote her name on the back of the page and waited for further instructions.

"In just a moment," Mr. Cooper explained, "Mr. Abiel and I will hand out the fish stamps, straws, paint, and paint brushes to each group. Once you have received all of the supplies, you can get started."

When Lucy received the supplies, she quickly started painting on one of the stamps. She remembered swimming in Kihei, Hawaii, last summer and seeing a variety of fish while snorkeling with her parents. One of her favourites was the reef triggerfish, which was different shades of blue and yellow.

Lucy held tightly onto the wooden handle on the back of the stamp and carefully placed it onto her page. When she lifted the stamp, a beautiful painting of a reef triggerfish was on her page. Lucy smiled and quickly reached for another stamp.

After placing two other fish onto her page, Lucy took a thin paintbrush. She dabbed the brush into green paint and began making seaweed. Some of it was tall and some were short. Some of the seaweed was skinny, while other pieces were thick.

Next, Lucy reached for a straw. She carefully placed the end of the straw into the blue paint, then tapped it repeatedly on the page, creating many bubbles across the painting.

Finally, Lucy took a medium-sized paintbrush and started making different sized oysters on the bottom of the ocean floor. In one of the larger oysters, Lucy carefully painted a large pearl.

When she was finished, Lucy stepped back and admired her painting. She was proud of her work! She also appreciated that Mr. Cooper did not tell students exactly how to create the painting. Lucy felt like she was given a lot of freedom to be creative and think of ideas on her own.

Satisfaction rushed over Lucy and she raised her hand in the air to show Mr. Cooper her masterpiece.

"That is a wonderful painting! I especially like that you made a pearl in this oyster. What a neat idea!" Mr. Cooper said.

Chapter Takeaway

Learning will be (and should be) loud and messy at times!

Core Competency Challenge

Do not always show your students an example when completing projects. Instead, give them a rough outline of what is expected, and then sit back and be amazed at the sense of pride and joy students show when they finish a project.

Thoughts for Educators

- When we give students freedom to create projects on their own, they might be messy; however, when all is said and done, students can be proud because their work is their own.

- Try to make each guest in your classroom feel welcome. Write your guests a card, give them a gift, and encourage your students to clap and say "thank you" to each person who helps in the classroom.

Thoughts for Parents

- Your child needs to hear praise from you. Consider the following:
  1. Be genuine: Your child needs to know that you really mean what you are saying. Look them in the eyes and speak slowly.
  2. Be specific: Avoid broad statements such as "Good job" or "Well done." Instead, let your child know exactly what you like about something they have done.
  3. Praise effort: Instead of focusing on ability, praise your child's effort when they complete a project or task. When you focus on ability, e.g. "You are so smart!" that encourages a fixed mindset, which can teach that "I am either good at something or not." However, when you focus on effort, e.g. "Thank you for giving your best effort during soccer practice!" this will encourage a "growth mindset," which says "With time and effort, I can accomplish this task."
  4. Avoid comparison: Try not to compare your child to other children, e.g. "You are much faster than Tony." Instead, focus on your child and encourage their own talents and abilities.[28]

Suggested Readings Based on this Core Competency:

Beautiful Oops by Barney Saltzberg
Ish by Peter H. Reynolds
The Dot by Peter H. Reynolds

---

[28] "6 Proven Ways To Encourage Kids Effectively (Without Side Effects)," Parenting for Brain, accessed June 27, 2019, www.parentingforbrain.com/words-of-encouragement-for-kids/.

14

Paper Chains

Personal Awareness and Responsibility: I can set realistic goals, use strategies to accomplish them, and persevere with challenging tasks.

Don't be afraid to try something. If it fails, you can always
try again and again until you succeed. -Sonya Parker

Before she knew it, Mr. Cooper was packing up his art supplies and saying goodbye to the class. Lucy waved at Mr. Cooper as he walked into the hallway and hoped she would see him again soon.

"Class," Mr. Abiel announced, "we are going to begin our last lesson for the day. For STEM,[29] we are going to complete a project that we worked on last week. We are doing this to reflect on our thinking and come up with ideas to complete the task in a better way."

"If you have forgotten about the challenge, let me remind you. Your group will be given an eleven by seventeen sheet of paper. Your job is to create the longest paper chain possible with the piece of paper you have been given. At the end of the class, we will measure the chains and see if there have been improvements from last week."

---

[29] The term STEM, which stands for Science, Technology, Engineering and Math, was devised in 2001 by Dr. Judith Ramaley. Judith Hallinen, "An Overview of STEM Education," accessed November 18, 2019, https://www.britannica.com/topic/STEM-education.

"At this point," Mr. Abiel said, "I will give your group a few minutes to discuss how you are going to complete the challenge. Think about different strategies and who will be completing certain tasks such as cutting or taping loops together."

Without hesitation, Lucy turned to her group and said, "When we are cutting the paper, we need to cut it into thin strips. Last time, our group cut the strips into thick pieces and we quickly ran out of paper."

"Good point," Linda said. "I also think it will work well if we have two group members attaching the loops from opposite sides."

"Great idea!" Tony said.

Once all of the groups had discussed strategy, Mr. Abiel said, "We will be starting in five seconds. Remember to include everyone in your group, persevere when things become difficult, and have lots of fun! Five, four, three, two, one…go!"

Lucy looked up and saw that Mr. Abiel had given the class twelve minutes on a timer. It seemed like a lot of time, however, Lucy knew it would be over in the blink of an eye.

"Linda and I can tape the loops together if you would like to start cutting thin strips of paper. How does that sound, Tony?"

"Sounds good to me!" Tony said.

As time went on, Linda said, "We only have five minutes left and we haven't even used half the piece of paper. Maybe you should cut the strips a little thicker, Tony."

"I was just thinking the same thing," Tony said. "I also noticed that it hasn't been easy for you to tape the loops together because the strips of paper are so skinny. I will try to make them a little thicker."

Mr. Abiel walked over to the group and praised them for their collaboration. "I appreciate how you are working well together as a group. You realized that your original plan was not working and have made plans to change things for the remainder of the challenge. Well done, everyone!"

"Thanks, Mr. Abiel!" Lucy said. "It's been difficult at times, but we think that this chain will be longer than the one we made last week!"

Before long, Mr. Abiel was counting down. "We are finished in three seconds, everyone. Three, two, one. That's it. Please place your hands in the air. I will come and collect the chains from each group."

Lucy, Tony, and Linda smiled at each other. They had worked hard and felt proud of themselves for pushing through when things got tough.

Mr. Abiel collected the chains from each group and attached them to the whiteboard using strong magnets.

"The first thing I want to show you," Mr. Abiel said, "is a picture from last week." He loaded a picture on the Smart Board of all the chains from last week's challenge. "Does anyone notice a difference from last week's chains to the chains we made today?"

Lucy looked hard at the picture for a moment and quickly noticed a big difference. She put her hand in the air, and Mr. Abiel asked Lucy to share her thoughts with the class.

"Last week," Lucy explained, "there was only one chain long enough to touch the floor. However, this week, every chain is touching the floor because the strips of paper are much skinnier."

"I noticed the exact same thing," Mr. Abiel said. "What this shows me is that you all reflected on the challenge from last week and learned from your experience. This is a very valuable lesson. You are all going to face challenging tasks in your life. If you make a mistake or don't complete the task as well as you would have liked to, don't give up. I encourage all of you to learn from your mistakes. Take time to reflect on your experiences. Think about what went well and what didn't go well. And then, try to complete the task again. You will be amazed at what you can accomplish when you try and try and try again!"

Chapter Takeaway

Reflection is a key part of learning. It can be easy to give up when things become difficult or we face failure. However, we want our students to learn from their mistakes and keep trying until they see growth in their talents and abilities.

Core Competency Challenge

Have students complete a challenge multiple times. Each time, provide an opportunity for students to reflect on their experience and determine how they can improve in the future. Think depth over breadth!

Thoughts for Educators

- Talk to your students about having a "growth mindset." Class Dojo has wonderful videos that explain this concept clearly.[30]
- It can be easy to focus on covering lots of things and leave little to no time for reflection. As educators, we need to give our students time to think about their experiences and provide opportunities for them to try again.

Thoughts for Parents

- Talk to your child about mistakes you have made and how you have learned from them. Growth happens when we have the courage to take risks and learn from our experiences.
- Consider the phrase, "More is caught than taught."[31] When you face a challenging task, how do you respond? Your child is likely watching and learning from your actions.

Suggested Readings Based on this Core Competency

How to Find A Fox by Nilah Magruder
What Do You Do with A Problem? by Kobi Yamada

---

[30] "ClassDojo," accessed June 28, 2019, https://ideas.classdojo.com/.
[31] Rachel Cruze, "Your Kids and Money: More Is Caught Than Taught," Dave Ramsey, accessed June 27, 2019, www.daveramsey.com/blog/more-is-caught-than-taught.

15

If You Can Hear Me

Social Awareness and Responsibility: I can be
part of a group and invite others to join.

Let us remember: One book, one pen, one child,
and one teacher can change the world.
-Malala Yousafzai

As soon as Lucy and her classmates had cleaned up from the STEM challenge, Mr. Abiel said, "I am going to be looking to see which group is ready for our end of the day routine. Once I dismiss your group, please stack your chair and meet me at the blue carpet."

Lucy folded her hands on top of her desk and smiled at Mr. Abiel. Her group was quickly dismissed, and, after stacking her chair, Lucy sat at the very front of the carpet, closest to Mr. Abiel's chair.

When everyone had gathered, Mr. Abiel asked, "Are there any song requests today?"

"If You're Happy and You Know It?" Linda said.

"Of course!" Mr. Abiel said. Without hesitating, he grabbed his black guitar, named Gus, from a wooden stand and started strumming the chords to the song. Soon, the entire class was singing:

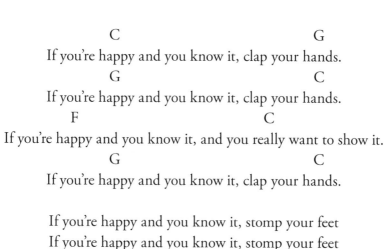

<pre>
                  C   G
    If you're happy and you know it, clap your hands.
                  G   C
    If you're happy and you know it, clap your hands.
                F   C
  If you're happy and you know it, and you really want to show it.
                  G   C
    If you're happy and you know it, clap your hands.
</pre>

<pre>
      If you're happy and you know it, stomp your feet
      If you're happy and you know it, stomp your feet
  If you're happy and you know it, and you really want to show it.
      If you're happy and you know it, stomp your feet.[32]
</pre>

As Mr. Abiel played the last chord, he softly said, "Okay everyone, it's time for 'If You Can Hear Me.[33]' Remember, if you see someone being left out during the song, do your best to include them. We want everyone to know they are a valued part of our classroom community!"

Mr. Abiel smiled at the class and started to sing:

<pre>
          G C D   C   G
    If you can hear me, can you wave your hands in the air.
</pre>

Immediately, students began to wave their hands back and forth. Mr. Abiel continued:

<pre>
          G   C D   C   G
    If you can hear me, can you give a friend a high five.
</pre>

---

[32] Joe Ranoso, "If You're Happy and You Know It."

[33] I wrote this song while teaching a Grade One class. If readers would like to use this song, they may do so, provided they credit me.

Students quickly found a classmate at the carpet and gave one another a high five.

Mr. Abiel sang:

G C D   C   G
If you can hear me, can you say "Have a good night" to a friend.

Students loudly spoke to one another until Mr. Abiel said, "I'm looking for students who are sitting nicely at the carpet. Once I say your name, you can grab your water bottle, put on your coat, and line up at the door with your backpack."

He continued by singing: "Ava, Violet, Tony, and Lucy."

Once Lucy heard her name, she stood up and started getting ready to go home.

Chapter Takeaway

We all want to feel like we belong no matter where we are and who we are with. As educators, we have the awesome privilege of creating strong classroom environments where everyone feels like they belong. Let's take this responsibility seriously and strive to help everyone know they are noticed and valued.

Core Competency Challenge

At the end of each day, have an activity that helps everyone feel like they are a valued part of the classroom community. For example, try singing a song or leading students through a simple game where everyone is invited to participate.

Thoughts for Educators

- If you have a musical instrument in your classroom, ask your students to name it for you. You can name your instrument and teach a graphing lesson at the same time by having students vote.

- Try writing songs or chants for your students. You might be surprised how well students remember words when they are paired with a catchy jingle!

Thoughts for Parents

- Discuss why it is important to participate in activities inside and outside of the classroom, e.g. "You can learn from others and others can learn from you!"
- Brainstorm ideas for how your family can make the world a better place, e.g. cleaning up a park, baking cookies and sharing them with others, writing encouraging notes to the principal, and many more ways!

Suggested Reading Based on this Core Competency

Kindness is Cooler, Mrs. Ruler by Margery Cuyler

16

See You Later

Once Lucy had her water bottle, coat, and backpack, she lined up and began talking with Ava.

"Do you want to play at the park after school?"

"I sure would!" Ava said. "I'll just need to check with my mom first."

"Me too," Lucy replied. "But I'm guessing my mom will let me."

As Lucy was talking with Ava, Mr. Abiel announced, "Thank you for a great day, everyone! I love you and want everyone to know that I really enjoy teaching our class. Before you head home today, I just wanted to remind you of a few things that are happening tomorrow. We will be having Fruit and Veggie Friday, our spelling test, and hot lunch."

Mr. Abiel continued, "When we get downstairs, don't forget to say 'See you later' to me before leaving with your parents. I will now wait to see which line is ready."

Everyone quickly straightened up and looked expectantly at Mr. Abiel. After a few moments, Mr. Abiel said, "Girls, let's go first!"

Lucy followed Mr. Abiel down the green staircase with the rest of her class. As she neared the bottom of the stairs, Lucy saw her mom and waved frantically at her. Lucy's mom smiled and waved back.

"See you later, Mr. Abiel!" Lucy said.

"See you tomorrow, Lucy."

Without a moment to lose, Lucy dashed towards her mom and loudly asked, "Mom! Can I play at the park with Ava? Please, Mom? Please?"

Lucy's mom laughed and said, "Slow down. How about we start with 'Hi Mom, how was your day?'"

"Sorry," Lucy mumbled. "Hi Mom, did you have a good day?"

"I did, thank you. Now, in regards to playing at the park, yes, that is okay with me. However, when I say it is time to leave, you need to listen to me the first time."

"Okay!" Lucy said. "Thanks, Mom!"

Lucy quickly spun around and tried to find Ava in the crowd of people. Before long, she locked eyes with Ava and shouted, "Ava, I can play at the park. What about you?"

"Yes, I can!" Ava said. "Come on, let's go!"

17

A Flower Blooms

The girls had a wonderful time together at the park. They played on the monkey bars and took turns pushing one another on the swing set. All too soon, however, Lucy's mom said, "Alright, Lucy, it's time for us to go. Your dad is expecting us at home soon for a special birthday supper."

"Okay, Mom." Lucy replied. "See you tomorrow, Ava."

"See you then," Ava said.

Before long, Lucy was on her way home with her mom.

"Mom?" Lucy asked.

"Yes, dear?"

"What has four wheels and flies?"

"Hmmm..." said Mom. "I'm not sure. What has four wheels and flies?"

"A garbage truck!" Lucy said.

"That's a good one! Now, I have one for you. What do you call tiny waves at the beach?"

Lucy thought for a few moments before saying, "I don't know."

"Microwaves!" Mom giggled.

"I am definitely telling Ava that joke tomorrow," Lucy said. "I'm pretty sure she has never heard that one before."

When Ava and her mom walked through the front door of their house, they were hit with a delightful smell coming from the kitchen.

"Welcome home!" Dad said.

"What are you cooking?" Mom inquired. "It smells divine!"

"My famous beef bourguignon!" Dad said. "Everything will be ready shortly. Why don't you both get changed and meet me in the kitchen when you are finished."

After changing out of her uniform, Lucy walked back downstairs into the kitchen.

"Hi, dear," Dad said. "What was the best part of your day?"

"My favourite part was probably a fish painting we made." Lucy said. "A nice man named Mr. Cooper came to our class and helped us with the project."

"That sounds like a lot of fun!" Dad said. "We'll have to hang your painting up in the house when you bring it home."

Before long, Lucy and her parents were eating a delicious meal together.

"This is really good!" Lucy said. "What's the secret ingredient?"

"Do you promise not to tell anyone?" Dad asked.

"Of course!"

"The secret ingredient is...bacon!"

Lucy laughed. "Of course it is! Bacon makes everything taste better!"

After supper, Lucy's dad brought out a black forest cake with a single candle on top. Lucy and her father loudly sang "Happy Birthday" out of tune. Lucy's mom laughed and blew out the candle with ease.

After eating the cake, Lucy and her parents decided to play Yahtzee. They played three rounds and Lucy's mom rolled a Yahtzee two times!

When the game was finished, Lucy's mom said, "This has been a wonderful birthday. Thank you both for making this day so special!"

"You're welcome, Mom!" Lucy said.

"Although I don't want this night to end, I think it's time for you to start getting ready for bed, Lucy."

"Do I have to?" Lucy asked.

"I'm afraid so," Mom said. "Tonight is a school night and you will need your energy for tomorrow."

"Okay, I'll start getting ready soon. But before I do, I just wanted to give you one more thing for your birthday."

Lucy raced over to her backpack and began rummaging through it. When she found her journal, she proudly brought it over to her mom and explained, "I wrote a story for you at school today. Before you go to bed, could you read it?"

"I can certainly do that," Mom said, before placing the journal on a wooden coffee table. "Now, come on. Let's head upstairs and get ready for bed."

After Lucy had changed into her pajamas and brushed her teeth, she climbed into bed. Her mom and dad said a short prayer with Lucy before turning out the lamp at her bedside.

"Good night," Mom whispered. "We love you and couldn't be more proud of you."

"Good night, Mom. Good night, Dad. I love you, too," Lucy whispered.

After gently closing her door, Dad said, "I think I'm going to watch a little T.V. Care to join me?"

"I will join you soon," Mom said. "Before I come, I would like to read Lucy's story."

"Sounds good, dear. See you soon."

When Lucy's mom got downstairs, she picked up the journal and sat down on a brown leather couch in the living room. She carefully read each word that Lucy had written earlier in the day. When she reached the end of the story, a large smile began to spread across her face. And as her smile widened, a pink lily sitting in a vase on the kitchen counter slowly began to bloom.

Epilogue

In his book, "*Creative Schools: The Grassroots Revolution That's Transforming Education*," Sir Ken Robinson writes:

> I've said that education is a living process that can best be compared to agriculture. Gardeners know that they don't make plants grow. They don't attach roots, glue the leaves, and paint the petals. Plants grow themselves. The job of the gardener is to create the best conditions for that to happen. Good gardeners create those conditions, and poor ones don't. It's the same with teaching. Good teachers create the conditions for learning, and poor ones don't. Good teachers also know that they are not always in control of these conditions.[34]

As educators and parents, let's be committed to creating positive environments for children to thrive. Nobody said it would be easy. There will be challenges and setbacks: however, the result will amaze you!

I believe we can learn a great deal from plants when it comes to children. I understand that children and plants are very different; however, there are a few things we can apply to children from learning about ideal conditions for plants. Consider the following:

Patience: Plants take time to grow. I know that this sounds obvious, however, it can be challenging to be patient when you are excited about

---

[34] Ken Robinson and Lou Aronica, *Creative Schools: The Grassroots Revolution That's Transforming Education*. (New York: Penguin Books, 2015), 102.

eating fruits and vegetables from your garden. I believe the same is true with children. We are excited to see them reading, writing, spelling, solving problems, coming up with creative ideas, etc. However, learning takes time. When we understand this, I feel we will put less pressure on children and give them the time and space they need to grow.

Support: There are many kinds of plants, e.g. tomatoes and peas, that need support in order to thrive. Without support, these plants would quickly fall over and not be able to reach their full potential. Children also need our support. They need to have a village of people around them that will guide them throughout their life.

Sunshine: We have heard since childhood that plants need plenty of sunshine in order to survive. Sunshine helps with the process of photosynthesis, where plants are able to make food through sunlight, carbon dioxide, and water. When I think of sunshine, I think of the word warmth. Our kids need warmth in their lives to thrive. They need to have someone who notices them, smiles at them, hugs them, laughs with them, and cries with them. I encourage you to think of ways in which you can share warmth with children in your own life.

Soil: Soil provides plants with a base for roots to grow into. Soil also provides essential nutrients that plants need. If you have ever had a plant that started to wilt, maybe you added some fertilizer to the soil. Often, the plant begins to grow and produce fruit once again. When I think of the word soil, the word dirt also comes to mind. I believe that children need to get dirty in order to bloom. This means that they should not be afraid to make mistakes, or to try something new and learn from their experience, whether positive or negative. I also believe this means that children actually need to get dirty. They need to place their hands in dirt, get sap on their clothes from climbing trees, and jump into large piles of leaves. How else can they explore and make an emotional attachment to the world? Ask yourself, would I rather learn about a tree from a textbook or actually go outside and use my hands to feel the rough bark of a tree? Listen to a tree's leaves blow in the wind? Smell the fragrance of its flowers? Taste the sweet fruit it produces? Observe the size of a tree's trunk? I certainly know my answer!

Water: Without water, plants quickly shrivel up. This is because essential nutrients are unable to travel throughout the plant. When I think of water, the term refreshment comes to mind. Think for a moment of a washcloth that is used for washing dishes. When a washcloth is placed in water, it becomes saturated. However, when we wring the cloth out, it is empty and dry. The same process happens with children. When children come to school, they use a lot of energy to learn a variety of skills and concepts. At the end of the day, students have been wrung out and need time to be refreshed. This can happen in a number of ways. Children need to eat healthy meals, get plenty of sleep, have time for unstructured play, and participate in moments of silence. I encourage you to provide time for children to slow down so they can absorb everything they need to learn.

Appendix 1

Complete List of Core Competencies

The following is a complete list of profiles from the Government of British Columbia's website.

Communicating

Profile One
In a safe and supported environment, I respond meaningfully to communication from peers and adults.

Profile Two
In familiar settings, I communicate with peers and adults.

I talk and listen to people I know. I can communicate for a purpose. I can understand and share basic information about topics that are important to me, and answer simple, direct questions about my activities and experiences.

Profile Three
I communicate purposefully, using forms and strategies I have practiced.

I participate in conversations for a variety of purposes (e.g., to connect, help, be friendly, learn and share). I listen and respond to others. I can consider my purpose when I am choosing a form and content. I can communicate clearly about topics I know and understand well, using forms and strategies I have practiced. I gather the basic information I need and present it.

Profile Four
I communicate clearly and purposefully, using a variety of forms appropriately.

I share my ideas and try to connect them with others' ideas. I am an active listener – I make connections and ask clarifying and extending questions when appropriate. I can plan ways to make my message clear and engaging for my audience and create communications that focus on a variety of purposes and audiences. I acquire the information I need for specific tasks and for my own interests and present it clearly.

Profile Five
I communicate confidently, using forms and strategies that show attention to my audience and purpose.

In discussions and conversations, I am focused and help to build and extend understanding. I am an engaged listener; I ask thought-provoking questions when appropriate and integrate new information. I can create a wide range of effective communications that feature powerful images and words, and I identify ways to change my communications to make them effective for different audiences. I use my understanding of the role and impact of story to engage my audiences in making meaning. I acquire information about complex and specialized topics from various sources, synthesize it, and present it with thoughtful analysis.

Profile Six
I communicate with intentional impact, in well-constructed forms that are effective in terms of my audience and in relation to my purpose.

I contribute purposefully to discussions and conversations. I synthesize, deepen, and transform my own and others' thinking. I can weave multiple messages into my communications; I understand that my audience will use their own knowledge and experiences in making meaning. I show understanding and control of the forms and technologies I use; I can assess audience response and draw on a repertoire of strategies to increase my intended impact. I can acquire, critically analyze, and integrate well-chosen information from a range of sources.

Collaborating
Profile One
In familiar situations, I can participate with others.

Profile Two
In familiar situations, I cooperate with others for specific purposes.
I contribute during group activities, cooperate with others, and listen respectfully to their ideas. I can work with others for a specific purpose.

Profile Three
I contribute during group activities with peers and share roles and responsibilities to achieve goals.
I take on different roles and tasks in the group and work respectfully and safely in our shared space. I express my ideas and help others feel comfortable to share theirs so that all voices are included. I work with others to achieve a common goal and can evaluate our group processes and results.

Profile Four
I can confidently interact and build relationships with other group members to further shared goals.
I can identify and apply roles and strategies to facilitate group work. I draw on past experiences to negotiate and develop group processes. I am an active listener and speaker. I share my ideas and try to connect them with others' ideas, I ask clarifying questions and check for understanding when appropriate, and I test my ideas with others and consider their input. I help resolve conflicts and challenges as they arise. I recognize how my contributions and those of others complement each other. I can plan with others and adjust our plan according to the group's purpose.

Profile Five
I can facilitate group processes and encourage collective responsibility for our progress.
I play a role in collectively monitoring the progress of the group and adjust my contributions as needed. I recognize the interdependence

of our roles and draw on these to move us forward. I ask thought-provoking questions, integrate new information and various perspectives from others, and think critically about whose voices are missing. I can disagree respectfully, and I anticipate potential conflicts and help manage them when they arise. I give, receive, and act on constructive feedback in support of our goals, and I can evaluate and revise plans with other group members.

Profile Six
I can connect my group with other groups and broader networks for various purposes.
I can step outside of my comfort zone to develop working relationships with unfamiliar groups. I develop and coordinate networking partnerships beyond and in service of the group. I demonstrate my commitment to the group's purpose by taking on different roles as needed. I acknowledge different perspectives and seek out and create space for missing or marginalized voices. I summarize key themes to identify commonalities and focus on deepening or transforming our collective thinking and actions. I recognize when wisdom and strategies from others are needed and access these to address complex goals. I help create connections with other groups or networks to further our common goals and our impact.

Creative Thinking
Profile One
I get ideas when I play.

I get ideas when I use my senses to explore. My play ideas are fun for me and make me happy. I make my ideas work or I change what I am doing.

Profile Two
I can get new ideas or build on or combine other people's ideas to create new things within the constraints of a form, a problem, or materials.

I can get new ideas to create new things or solve straightforward problems. My ideas are fun, entertaining, or useful to me and my peers, and I have a sense of accomplishment. I can use my imagination to get new ideas of my own, or build on other's ideas, or combine other people's ideas in new ways. I can usually make my ideas work within the constraints of a given form, problem, or materials if I keep playing with them.

Profile Three
I can get new ideas in areas in which I have an interest and build my skills to make them work.

I generate new ideas as I pursue my interests. I deliberately learn a lot about something by doing research, talking to others, or practicing, so that I can generate new ideas about it; the ideas often seem to just pop into my head. I build the skills I need to make my ideas work, and I usually succeed, even if it takes a few tries.

Profile Four
I can get new ideas or reinterpret others' ideas in novel ways.

I get ideas that are new to my peers. My creative ideas are often a form of self-expression for me. I have deliberate strategies for quieting my conscious mind (e.g., walking away for a while, doing something relaxing, being deliberately playful), so that I can be more creative. I use my experiences with various steps and attempts to direct my future work.

Profile Five
I can think "outside the box" to get innovative ideas and persevere to develop them.

I can get new ideas that are innovative, may not have been seen before, and have an impact on my peers or in my community. I have interests and passions that I pursue over time. I look for new perspectives, new problems, or new approaches. I am willing to take significant risks in my thinking in order to generate lots of ideas. I am willing to accept ambiguity, setbacks, and failure, and I use them to advance the development of my ideas.

Profile Six
I can develop a body of creative work over time in an area of interest or passion.

I can get ideas that are groundbreaking or disruptive and can develop them to form a body of work over time that has an impact in my community or beyond. I challenge assumptions as a matter of course and have deliberate strategies (e.g., free writing or sketching, meditation, thinking in metaphors and analogies) for getting new ideas intuitively. I have a strong commitment to a personal aesthetic and values, and the inner motivation to persevere over years if necessary to develop my ideas.

Critical and Reflective Thinking
Profile One
I can explore.

I can explore materials and actions. I can show whether I like something or not.

Profile Two
I can use evidence to make simple judgments.

I can ask questions, make predictions, and use my senses to gather information. I can explore with a purpose in mind and use what I learn. I can tell or show others something about my thinking. I can contribute to and use simple criteria. I can find some evidence and make judgments. I can reflect on my work and experiences and tell others about something I learned.

Profile Three
I can ask questions and consider options. I can use my observations, experience, and imagination to draw conclusions and make judgments.

I can ask open-ended questions, explore, and gather information. I experiment purposefully to develop options. I can contribute to and use criteria. I use observation, experience, and imagination to draw conclusions, make judgments, and ask new questions. I can describe my thinking and how it is changing. I can establish goals individually and with others. I can connect my learning with my experiences, efforts, and goals. I give and receive constructive feedback.

Profile Four

I can gather and combine new evidence with what I already know to develop reasoned conclusions, judgments, or plans.

I can use what I know and observe to identify problems and ask questions. I explore and engage with materials and sources. I can develop or adapt criteria, check information, assess my thinking, and develop reasoned conclusions, judgments, or plans. I consider more than one way to proceed and make choices based on my reasoning and what I am trying to do. I can assess my own efforts and experiences and identify new goals. I give, receive, and act on constructive feedback.

Profile Five

I can evaluate and use well-chosen evidence to develop interpretations; identify alternatives, perspectives, and implications; and make judgments. I can examine and adjust my thinking.

I can ask questions and offer judgments, conclusions, and interpretations supported by evidence I or others have gathered. I am flexible and open-minded; I can explain more than one perspective and consider implications. I can gather, select, evaluate, and synthesize information. I consider alternative approaches and make strategic choices. I take risks and recognize that I may not be immediately successful. I examine my thinking, seek feedback, reassess my work, and adjust. I represent my learning and my goals and connect these with my previous experiences. I accept constructive feedback and use it to move forward.

Profile Six

I can examine evidence from various perspectives to analyze and make well-supported judgments about and interpretations of complex issues.

I can determine my own framework and criteria for tasks that involve critical thinking. I can compile evidence and draw reasoned conclusions. I consider perspectives that do not fit with my understandings. I am open-minded and patient, taking the time to explore, discover, and understand. I make choices that will help me create my intended impact on an audience or situation. I can place my work and that of others in a broader context. I can connect the results of my inquiries and analyses with action. I can articulate a keen awareness of my strengths, my aspirations and how my experiences and contexts affect my frameworks and criteria. I can offer detailed analysis, using specific terminology, of my progress, work, and goals.

Personal Awareness and Responsibility

Profile One
I can show a sense of accomplishment and joy, and express some wants, needs, and preferences. I can sometimes recognize my emotions.

Profile Two
I can initiate actions that bring me joy and satisfaction and recognize that I play a role in my well-being.

I can seek out experiences that make me feel happy and proud. I can express my wants and needs and celebrate my efforts and accomplishments. I have some strategies that help me recognize and manage my feelings and emotions. I recognize and can explain my role in learning activities and explorations, and I can give some evidence of my learning. I can describe how some specific choices can affect my well-being and participate in activities that support my well-being.

Profile Three
I can make choices that help me meet my wants and needs and increase my feelings of well-being. I take responsibility for my actions.

I can take action toward meeting my own wants and needs and finding joy and satisfaction, and work toward a goal or solving a problem. I can use strategies that increase my feeling of well-being and help me manage my feelings and emotions. I can connect my actions with both positive and negative consequences and try to make adjustments; I accept feedback. I make decisions about my activities and take some responsibility for my physical and emotional well-being.

Profile Four
I can recognize my strengths and take responsibility for using strategies to focus, manage stress, and accomplish my goals.

I advocate for myself and my ideas; I accept myself. I am willing to engage with ideas or information that is challenging for me. I can be focused and determined. I can set realistic goals, use strategies to accomplish them, and persevere with challenging tasks. I can tell when I am becoming angry, upset, or frustrated, and I have strategies to calm myself. I can make choices that benefit my well-being and keep me safe in the communities I belong to.

Profile Five
I recognize my value and advocate for my rights. I take responsibility for my choices, my actions, and my achievements.

I have valuable ideas to share. I am willing to explore controversial issues, and I can imagine and work toward change in myself and in the world. I can set priorities; implement, monitor, and adjust a plan; and assess the results. I take responsibility for my learning, seeking help as I need it. I use strategies for working toward a healthy and balanced lifestyle, for dealing with emotional challenges, and for finding peace in stressful times. I know how to find the social support I need.

Profile Six
I can identify my strengths and limits, find internal motivation, and act on opportunities for self-growth. I take responsibility for making ethical decisions.

I am aware of my personal journey and reflect on my experiences as a way of enhancing my well-being and dealing with challenges. I can advocate for myself in stressful situations. I can take the initiative to inform myself about controversial issues and take ethical positions. I take ownership of my goals, learning, and behaviour. I act on what is best, over time, in terms of my goals and aspirations. I recognize the implications of my choices and consult with others who may be affected by my decisions. I can identify my potential as a leader in the communities I belong to. I sustain a healthy and balanced lifestyle.

Positive Personal and Cultural Identity

Profile One
I am aware of myself as different from others.

I know my name. I am aware of some of my family and/or caregiver relationships.

Profile Two
I am aware of different aspects of myself. I can identity people, places, and things that are important to me.

With some help, I can identify some of my attributes. I can identify objects or images that represent things that are important to me and explain what I like and dislike. I can describe my family, home, and/or community (people and/or place).

Profile Three
I can describe different aspects of my identity.

I can identify my individual characteristics and explain what interests me. I can describe different groups that I belong to.

Profile Four
I have pride in who I am. I understand that I am a part of larger communities.

I can describe and demonstrate pride in my positive qualities, characteristics, and/or skills. I can explain why I make specific choices. I am able to represent aspects of my cultural contexts (such as family, communities, school, peer groups) through words and/or images, and describe some ways that I participate in, or am connected to, a community.

Profile Five
I understand that my identity is influenced by many aspects of my life. I am aware that my values shape my choices and contribute to making me a unique individual.

I understand that my characteristics, qualities, strengths, and challenges make me unique and are an important part of the communities I belong to (including people and places). I understand that what I value influences the choices I make and how I present myself in various contexts (including online). I can explain how I am able to use my strengths to contribute in my home and/or communities.

Profile Six
I can identify how my life experiences have contributed to who I am; I recognize the continuous and evolving nature of my identity.

I can identify ways in which my strengths can help me meet challenges, and how my challenges can be opportunities for growth. I understand that I will continue to develop new skills, abilities, and strengths. I can describe how aspects of my life experiences, family history, background, and where I live (or have lived) have influenced my values and choices. I understand that my learning is continuous, my concept of self and identity will continue to evolve, and my life experiences may lead me to identify with new communities of people and/or place.

Social Awareness and Responsibility
Profile One
I can be aware of others and my surroundings.

I like to be with my family and friends. I can help and be kind. I can tell when someone is sad or angry and try to make them feel better. I am aware that other people can be different from me.

Profile Two
In familiar settings, I can interact with others and my surroundings respectfully.

I can build relationships and work and play cooperatively. I can participate in activities to care for and improve my social and physical surroundings. I use materials respectfully. I can solve some problems myself and ask for help when I need it. I listen to others' ideas and concerns. I can be part of a group and invite others to join. I can identify when something is unfair to me or to others.

Profile Three
I can interact with others and the environment respectfully and thoughtfully.

I can build and sustain relationships and share my feelings. I contribute to group activities that make my classroom, school, community, or natural world a better place. I can identify different perspectives on an issue, clarify problems, consider alternatives, and evaluate strategies. I can demonstrate respectful and inclusive behaviour with people I know. I can explain why something is fair or unfair.

Profile Four
I can take purposeful action to support others and the environment.

I can build relationships and be a thoughtful and supportive friend. I can identify ways my actions and the actions of others affect my community and the natural environment. I look for ways to make my classroom, school, community, or natural world a better place and identify small things I can do that could make a difference. I demonstrate respectful and inclusive behaviour in a variety of settings, and I recognize that everyone has something to offer.

Profile Five
I can advocate and take action for my communities and the natural world. I expect to make a difference.

I am aware of how others may feel and take steps to help them feel included. I maintain relationships with people from different generations. I work to make positive change in the communities I belong to and the natural environment. I can clarify problems or issues, generate multiple strategies, weigh consequences, compromise to meet the needs of others, and evaluate actions. I value differences; I appreciate that each person has unique gifts. I use respectful and inclusive language and behaviour, including in social media. I can advocate for others.

Profile Six
I can initiate positive, sustainable change for others and the environment.

I build and sustain positive relationships with diverse people, including people from different generations. I show empathy for others and adjust my behaviour to accommodate their needs. I advocate and take thoughtful actions to influence positive, sustainable change in my communities and in the natural world. I can analyze complex social or environmental issues from multiple perspectives and understand how I am situated in types of privilege. I act to support diversity and defend human rights and can identify how diversity is beneficial for the communities I belong to.[35]

---

[35] Government of British Columbia, "Core Competencies," accessed November 18, 2019, https://curriculum.gov.bc.ca/competencies.

Appendix 2

Bibliography

"6 Proven Ways to Encourage Kids Effectively (Without Side Effects)." Parenting for Brain, last modified September 15, 2019, www.parentingforbrain.com/words-of-encouragement-for-kids/.

Ball, Sandra. "Self-Assessment of Core Competencies," *Starting With the Beginning*, last modified December 7, 2017, https://startingwiththebeginning.wordpress.com/author/sandraball/.

Brassell, Danny. *Bringing Joy Back into the Classroom*. Huntington Beach: Shell Education, 2012.

Chambers, Yanique. "Infographic: Teaching Children How to Make Friends," Kiddie Matters, accessed June 26, 2019, www.kiddiematters.com/infographic-teaching-children-how-to-make-friends/.

Chapman, Gary and Ross Campbell. *The Five Love Languages of Children*. Chicago: Northfield Publishing, 2005.

"Class Dojo." Accessed June 27, 2019. https://ideas.classdojo.com/.

Cruze, Rachel. "Your Kids and Money: More Is Caught Than Taught," Dave Ramsey, accessed June 27, 2019, www.daveramsey.com/blog/more-is-caught-than-taught.

Cullham, Ruth. *6 + 1 Traits of Writing: The Complete Guide for Primary Grades*. New York: Scholastic Teaching Resources, 2005.

GoNoodle. Accessed June 27, 2019. www.gonoodle.com.

Government of British Columbia, "Core Competencies," accessed June 27, 2019, https://curriculum.gov.bc.ca/competencies.

Hallinen, Judith. "An Overview of STEM Education," accessed November 18, 2019, https://www.britannica.com/topic/STEM-education.

Holecko, Catherine. "Brain Break Ideas for Busy Kids," Verywell Family, accessed June 27, 2019, www.verywellfamily.com/brain-breaks-for-busy-kids-1257211.

"Kelso's Choice." Brownsburg Community School Corporation. Last accessed June 27, 2019. www.brownsburg.k12.in.us/Page/1287.

Kunesh, Tara. "Multiple Intelligence Test for Children," LoveToKnow, accessed June 27, 2019, https://kids.lovetoknow.com/wiki/Multiple_Intelligence_Test_for_Children.

Li, Waynee. "Buddy Bench to Help Children Make Friends at North Vancouver School," CBC, last modified March 30, 2016, www.cbc.ca/news/canada/british-columbia/buddy-bench-to-help-children-make-friends-at-north-vancouver-school-1.3512812.

matticeha1. "Tattling vs Telling Large," YouTube, February 25, 2012, https://www.youtube.com/watch?v=7H21_mkimkM.

Mayer, Jordan "If You Can Hear Me," January, 2017.

Means, Leslie. "50 Questions To Ask Your Kids Instead Of Asking How Was Your Day," Her View from Home, accessed June 27, 2019, https://herviewfromhome.com/50-questions-to-ask-your-kids-instead-of-asking-how-was-your-day/.

Munsch, Robert. *Ribbon Rescue*. Toronto: Scholastic Canada, 1999.

Oxford Learning. "Day or Night: When Is the Best Time To Study?" accessed November 18, 2019, https://www.oxfordlearning.com/best-time-day-to-study/.

Pallozzi, Kim. "I'm A Teacher And I Can See The Benefits Of Eye Contact In My Classroom," accessed October 29, 2019, https://www.cbc.ca/parents/learning/view/im-a-teacher-i-see-first-hand-kids-arent-making-eye-contact-these-days.

Pereira, Kate. "Why Should My Child Read?" Motivating Minds, accessed June 27, 2019, https://mrspereirasclass.weebly.com/why-should-my-child-read.html.

Peterson, Andrew, "He Gave Us Stories," Reformation Bible College, last modified July 23, 2015, www.youtube.com/watch?v=mNC3UuDOCgs.

Petit Journey. "10 Reasons A Daily Routine is Important for Your Child (and How to Set One)," Petit, last modified January 10, 2017, https://www.petitjourney.com.au/10-reasons-a-daily-routine-is-important-for-your-child-and-how-to-set-one/.

Raposo, Joe. "If You're Happy and You Know It."

Reitz, Nicholas. "GROUPS Poster," Teachers Pay Teachers, accessed June 27, 2019, www.teacherspayteachers.com/Product/GROUPS-Poster-1182282.

Robinson, Ken and Lou Aronica. *Creative Schools: The Grassroots Revolution That's Transforming Education*. New York: Penguin Books, 2015.

Sautter, Elizabeth. "Taking a Deeper Look at Whole Body Listening: It's a Tool Not a Rule," Social Thinking, accessed June 27, 2019, www.socialthinking.com/Articles?name=whole-body-listening-its-a-tool-not-a-rule.

Tabb, Lanesha. "Morning Work Binder for Empathy," accessed June 26, 2019, www.teacherspayteachers.com/Product/Morning-Work-Binder -for-Empathy-2495804.

The OT Toolbox. "Self-Reflection Activities for Kids," last modified March 6, 2018, www.theottoolbox.com/self-reflection-activities-for-kids/.

Teachers Resisting Unhealthy Children's Entertainment. "Family Play Plans," accessed June 27, 2019, www.truceteachers.org/family-play-plans.html.

Teachers Resisting Unhealthy Children's Entertainment. *TRUCE Play and Toy Guide*, TRUCE, March 2017. www.truceteachers.org/uploads/1/5/5/7/15571834/truce_play_and_toy_guide_2017_final_updated.pdf.

Manufactured by Amazon.ca
Bolton, ON

15640316R00062